W9-BSJ-437

THE NATIONAL AUDUBON SOCIETY COLLECTION
NATURE SERIES

NORTH AMERICAN
BUTTERFLIES

THE NATIONAL AUDUBON SOCIETY COLLECTION
NATURE SERIES™

NORTH AMERICAN
BUTTERFLIES

Josleen Wilson

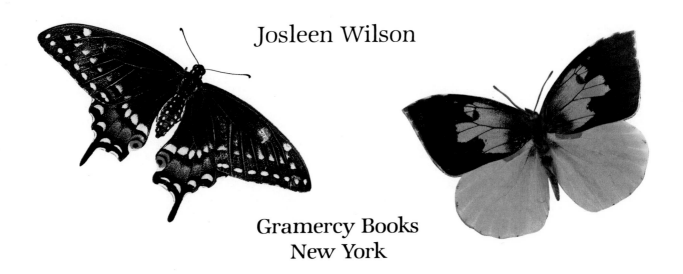

Gramercy Books
New York

All the photographs in this book are from Photo Researchers/National Audubon Society. The name of the individual photographer follows each caption.

Copyright © 1991 by Outlet Book Company, Inc.
All rights reserved

First published in 1991 by Gramercy Books,
distributed by Outlet Book Company, Inc.,
a Random House Company,
225 Park Avenue South,
New York, New York 10003

THE NATIONAL AUDUBON SOCIETY COLLECTION NATURE SERIES is a trademark
owned by the National Audubon Society, Inc.

Designed by Melissa Ring

Manufactured in Singapore

Library of Congress Cataloging in Publication Data
Wilson, Josleen.
   North Amerlcan butterflies / text by Josleen Wilson.
      p.   cm. — (The National Audubon Society collection nature
series)
   Includes index.
   ISBN 0-517-05023-4 :
   1. Butterflies—North America.   I. Title.   II. Series.
QL548.W55   1991
595.78′9097—dc20   91-11694
                                                     CIP

8   7   6   5   4   3   2   1

THE NATIONAL AUDUBON SOCIETY, incorporated in 1905, is one of the largest, most effective environmental groups in the world. Named after American Wildlife artist and naturalist, John James Audubon, the society has nearly 500,000 members in 500 chapters, nine regional and five state offices, and a government affairs center in Washington, D.C. Its headquarters are in New York City.

Audubon works on behalf of our natural heritage through scientific research, environmental education, and conservation action. It maintains a network of almost ninety wildlife sanctuaries nationwide and conducts both ecology camps for adults and youth programs for schoolchildren. Audubon publishes the leading conservation and nature magazine, *Audubon* and an ornithological journal, *American Birds*. It also publishes *Audubon Activist* and, as part of its youth program, *Audubon Adventures*. In addition, Audubon produces "World of Audubon" television specials, video cassettes and interactive discs, and other educational materials.

Audubon's mission as expressed by the "Audubon Cause" is to conserve native plants and animals and their habitats; to protect life from pollution, radiation, and toxic substances; to further the wise use of land and water; to seek solutions for global problems involving the interaction of populations, resources, and the environment; and to promote rational strategies for energy development and use, stressing conservation and renewable energy sources.

For further information regarding membership, write to the NATIONAL AUDUBON SOCIETY, 950 Third Avenue, New York, New York 10022.

CONTENTS

The World of Butterflies / 7

Papilionidae—Swallowtails and Parnassians / 27

Pieridae—Whites and Orangetips, Brimstones and Sulphurs / 35

Lycaenidae—Gossamer Wings / 41

Riodinidae—Metalmarks / 51

Libytheidae—The Snout Butterflies / 53

Nymphalidae—Brush-footed Butterflies / 55

Satyridae—Satyrs or Browns / 67

Danaidae—Milkweed Butterflies / 69

Hesperidae—Skippers / 73

Index / 79

THE WORLD OF BUTTERFLIES

In an alpine meadow, the air hums with the sound of insects busy in the undergrowth. White butterflies, wings splashed with scarlet and black, bejewel the tips of pink thistles. A breeze sways the tall grasses, and all across the surface of the meadow small bright wings flutter like flags in the air.

Butterflies, and their relatives the moths, unequaled in beauty and unrivaled in their fascination for scientists and nature lovers alike, make up a large group of insects known as the Lepidoptera (from the Greek words for "scale" and "wing"). Theirs is largely a distinction of convenience, for there are only a few superficial differences between butterflies and moths.

Butterflies fly by day, moths by night. Butterflies hold their colorful wings upright over their backs, moths hold their more muted wings flat. Butterflies have knobbed antennae, the antennae of moths are feathery. These "rules," however, are frequently flouted by individual species of both. There is no single feature that separates all butterflies from all moths.

CLASSIFYING BUTTERFLIES

The sheer numbers of species in the order Lepidoptera—somewhere between 140,000 and 165,000, with many species still unknown—bedevil lepidopterists who try to impose some kind of classification system.

The scientific method of classification has been developed over several centuries. Animals are classi-

A Clodius Parnassian *(Parnassius clodius)*, left, sips nectar from the flower of a thistle. The Ruddy Daggerwing *(Marpesia petreus)*, above, displays long, dashing tails on its hind wings. (Kjell B. Sandved)

fied into groups called phyla. Each phylum contains creatures which possess certain features in common. The phylum Arthropoda includes all those animals which have jointed limbs and a hard exoskeleton. A phylum is divided into classes. The largest class of the Arthropoda, and indeed the largest class in the animal kingdom, is the Insecta, to which the Lepidoptera belong.

Like all other insects, Lepidoptera have three main body divisions: head, thorax, and abdomen. They have six legs and one pair of antennae. Their hard skeletons wrap around the outside of their bodies.

Beyond these common features, insects are divided into twenty-nine orders. The Lepidoptera belong to a group of orders called the Endopterygota, winged insects whose life cycle progresses through four distinct stages. Beetles also belong to the Endopterygota.

An order, in this case Lepidoptera, is further subdivided into families, families into genera, and genera into species.

Some twenty thousand of these species are said to be butterflies. The most theatrically spangled are found in tropical lands below the equator. In North America today, even though much of the habitat in which butterflies and other insects thrive has been destroyed, there can be found seven hundred species of butterflies, ranging from the high mountain dwellers of the Arctic tundra to the languid flyers of subtropical Florida. Sometimes two different species are virtual look-alikes, although biologically they are different.

THE LIFE OF A BUTTERFLY

In the butterfly, as in other insects, behavior is, to a large extent, controlled by instinct. A butterfly has only a primitive brain, but a well-developed sympathetic nervous system. Gregariousness, flight behavior, and courtship are all largely determined by the butterfly's innate responses, which are built into its nervous system.

In its life cycle—which may last from a few weeks to more than a year—a butterfly goes through four different stages: egg; caterpillar; pupa, or chrysalis; and adult, or imago. When they are ready to mate, most adult butterflies dance elaborate courtship flights, the males using their striking colors to attract the females. During courtship, the male flutters around the female, waving his wings, and releasing a powerful aphrodesiac, called a pheromone, whose scent signals his eagerness to mate. When a female shows an interest in the male, they alight together, tapping each other with their antennae to detect other more subtle scents. The female holds her wings partly open and the male grasps her abdomen with his hind claspers so that their genitalia are linked together in the tail-to-tail position. The two butterflies remain linked, sometimes for several hours. If they are disturbed, they can fly while holding this position.

Immediately after mating, the female begins to search for a host plant that will ultimately feed her offspring. When she finds the right plant, she tests a leaf with her feet, which contain sense organs to help her detect the plant's suitability.

If she belongs to a species whose caterpillars feed on grass, the butterfly may release her eggs in flight, scattering them over a grassy meadow. Most of the time, however, she locates the proper plant, perches on a leaf, and then—curving her abdomen underneath—lays her eggs on the undersurface, where they will be protected from the weather and predators. Some females deposit one hundred eggs or more to ensure that some will survive to adulthood. The female secretes a sticky substance to cement the individual eggs to the plant.

The shape and texture of butterfly eggs vary in different species. The eggs may be round or oval, domed or flattened, smooth or heavily ribbed. The yolk of the egg supplies food as the young larva develops.

Eggs mature at different intervals, depending on the species and the climate. In temperate zones, for example, where there is a distinct seasonal change in

The mating of a male and female Woodland Skipper (*Ochlodes sylvanoides*). (R.J. Erwin)

climate, eggs laid in autumn often pass the winter in a resting stage. When mature, an egg often darkens in color, and a fully formed caterpillar is visible through the transparent shell.

THE EMERGING CATERPILLAR

The tiny caterpillar bites its way through the soft shell of the egg, using its jaws to cut a circle large enough for its head to fit through. The dark, hairy head emerges. At first, the caterpillar seems to be all head and jaws. Highly vulnerable to predators, it struggles, twisting and turning, to squeeze out of the egg. It braces its front legs against the leaf and pulls hard to finally free its weak body. As soon as it is out, the caterpillar consumes the eggshell, which contains nutrients essential for its growth.

As the caterpillar grows, it entirely fills its skin, which becomes very tight and rigid. To grow larger, it must discard its outer skin to expose a new, more elastic skin. A caterpillar may molt four or five times before reaching its maximum size, often changing color and appearance in the process.

Caterpillars are as varied and as colorful as adult butterflies. They may be smooth-skinned or fuzzy, spiny or long-haired, distinctively marked, brightly striped, or deceptively bland-looking. The head houses a primitive brain and sports short antennae. Caterpillars have small light-sensitive eyes called ocelli that are hard to see. Some species also have big false eyes, called eyespots, that look painted on. Whatever their outer appearance, each caterpillar carries the cells that will eventually produce an adult butterfly.

The caterpillar of the Tiger Swallowtail (*Papilio glaucus*), above, shows its false eyespots. (Jeff Lepore)

Preparing to pupate, an Anise Swallowtail (*Papilio zelicaon*) caterpillar, below, spins a silk girdle. (Jerome Wexler)

During this very active stage of life, species that depend on agricultural crops for food can be serious pests, chomping both plant flowers and foliage, often eating their way through entire fields of cultivated food crops. Fortunately, a few caterpillar species prefer weeds, and at least one carnivorous species, the Harvester (*Feniseca tarquinius*), consumes large quantities of aphids, which destroy crops. In these cases, their intense feeding activity can be quite beneficial to humans.

But life is not easy for growing caterpillars. Slow-moving and soft-bodied, caterpillars are easy fodder for birds, who nab them like peanuts to feed their young. To outwit the swooping, sharp-beaked predators, caterpillars use a large array of protective devices. For some, the large, weird-looking eyespots serve like Halloween makeup to scare away enemies. Others are shielded by their spiny coats, or their fat bodies are protected by long, dense hair. Some are camouflaged by their coloring, which perfectly matches the leaves they feed on, rendering them invisible to predators.

A few species have bright stripes that advertise an unpleasant surprise for would-be diners. These colorful caterpillars turn themselves into nasty pellets by feeding on poisonous plants. The caterpillars of the famous Monarch (*Danaus plexippus*), for example, feed on poisonous milkweeds. The caterpillars of the various longwing butterflies thrive on deadly passionflower vines. After one distasteful sampling, predators remember the distinct markings of these caterpillars and avoid similar look-alikes.

The caterpillars of many swallowtail butterflies have an unusual defense weapon they use when confronted by an enemy. The caterpillar rears up and from the back of its head inflates a Y-shaped gland, the osmeterium, which emits an unpleasant smell.

The caterpillar's industry and subterfuge is directed toward one great life event: metamorphosis. In its next manifestation, the butterfly enters a completely motionless stage of life, called the chrysalis, or pupa. The caterpillar must, however, first find a special place to pupate. It may be a concealed location where predators cannot easily see it, or—if it is a species whose crysalis is distasteful to predators—it may rest out in the open.

After the spot is found, the caterpillar grips a plant stem with its hind claspers and begins to spin silk from a spinneret below its head, weaving it into a small pad which adheres to the plant surface. Some caterpillars also weave a silk girdle around their bodies to help hold themselves in place. Caterpillars of many moths, and of a few species of butterfly, enter the soil and line hollow spots in the earth with silk to make a cocoon. Some make aboveground cocoons from leaves woven together with silk threads.

When the position is secured, the caterpillar begins to wriggle vigorously until the skin along its back splits. The casing of the chrysalis beneath shows through. As the caterpillar skin peels off, the chrysalis casing is exposed to the air and hardens. The pupa works the hooks on its tail securely into the silken pad. The digestive tract is emptied and the mouth and anus are sealed over. During the ensuing transformation the pupa neither eats nor drinks. In its final form, the chrysalis may hang straight down from the pad, or its head may be held upward by its silken girdle.

THE CHRYSALIS

The butterfly is now at its most vulnerable stage of life. Unable to move, its hope of survival depends on its ability to take on the shape and color of its surroundings. A chrysalis may look like a lifeless twig or a dead leaf. The most successful camouflage is created by an irregular shape that most easily blends in with the surroundings. Some chrysalises have ragged edges, others bristle with sharp spines that offer both camouflage and protection. Some have reflective spots to distract predators. The more brightly colored chrysalises, like their caterpillars, are only too ready to advertise their poisonous presence.

Depending on the species and the climate, the chrysalis will remain in its immobilized form for weeks or even months. Even though the pupa seems lifeless, amazing changes are taking place inside. When this stage is complete, the butterfly is fully grown within the nearly transparent chrysalis. The wings, antennae, and legs can be seen through the skin; color pigment appears in the wing scales, so even the pattern is clearly visible through the pupal case.

THE EMERGING BUTTERFLY

When the butterfly is ready to emerge, the upper part of its body swells, and the chrysalis splits along weak points behind the head. The butterfly takes in air and plumps up even further. Head and antennae emerge, followed by tightly folded wings and swollen abdomen. Once free of the chrysalis, the butterfly lets its wings hang down to gradually unfold with the help of gravity.

Each crumpled wing is composed of two thin sheets, or membranes, intricately bonded. Hollow veins lie between them. As blood drains down into the veins, the tiny folds flatten and, in a period of 10 to 20 minutes, the wings expand to full size. Here unfolded is a totally new creature, without any semblance to its former lives.

Small drops of excretory wastes, which have accumulated in the digestive tract during the pupal period, are ejected. These droplets are sometimes red, which led people in the Middle Ages to believe that emerging butterflies produced a "rain of blood."

The butterfly's outer skeleton is still soft and malleable. If the butterfly is damaged during its expansion stage—for example, if a human observer tries to hurry along the process by helping the butterfly unfold its wings—the unexpanded parts will harden and the butterfly will be crippled for life.

When the wings have reached full size the butterfly holds them apart for an hour or so, until they are completely dry and hardened. If it is evening, the butterfly will rest until the next day. After the wings are set, the butterfly opens and closes them, then takes to the air. The tough wing veins support the broad expanse of wing; muscles inside the thorax

The four stages of the Monarch *(Danaus plexippus)* life cycle: The tiny, delicately ribbed egg has a flat bottom. The brightly striped caterpillar has a pair of long filaments at the head and rear. Caterpillars feed on toxic milkweeds, which make them distasteful to birds. The jade-green chrysalis is trimmed with a half circle of gold studs. At first, the chrysalis is as hard as a green berry. As the butterfly develops inside, the case becomes transparent and the shape and colors of the adult butterfly can be clearly seen inside. When metamorphis is complete, the case splits behind the butterfly's head, and the fully formed adult butterfly, or imago, begins to emerge. Within twenty minutes the butterfly is completely free of the chrysalis. (Above, left to right: Richard F. Trump, Dr. A.G. Twomey, Jeanne White, Lee E. Battaglia.)

give the butterfly control over flight, allowing it to make sudden leaps and landings. The male butterfly usually flies straight to flowers for a first meal; the female will mate before eating.

Butterflies are their loveliest when they are freshly emerged. The newly emerged Nivalis Copper *(Epidemia nivalis)*, for example, has a lavender-rose upper surface, with gold underneath. Within a few days, its delicate coloring turns dingy as the tinted scales fall away. Similarly, the brilliant green of the Malachite *(Siproeta stelenes)* imago quickly fades when exposed to air and sun.

Before it can fly, the imago, right, lets its soft, crumpled wings hang down until they gradually unfold and the wing veins fill with blood. After an hour or so, the wings are dry and have hardened to their permanent shape. The imago will test its wings by opening and closing them once or twice, and then take to the air.
(J.H. Robinson)

THE ADULT BUTTERFLY

On the head of the new butterfly are a pair of antennae and a tightly coiled feeding tube, or proboscis.

The clubbed antennae, consisting of a series of rings or segments, are sense organs used for smelling and balance. Located in the base of each antenna is a special organ, called Johnston's organ, which helps the insect orient itself during flight.

Unlike caterpillars, butterflies have no jaws and must always take their food in liquid form, rolling out the long, hollow proboscis like a straw to probe deep into flowers and sip nectar and water. Butterflies may also drink honeydew, the sweet secretion produced by aphids, or the juice of decaying fruit, or even the liquids secreted from carrion. It is a common sight, especially in the tropics, to see a group of butterflies drinking from wet riverbanks.

On each side of the proboscis is a palp. The butterfly uses its palps, which are thickly covered with scales and sensory hairs, to examine its food before drinking.

The butterfly has two large compound eyes, made up of many individual lenses, or facets. The insect sees the world as a mosaic, each tiny picture created by a single facet. Although inferior to human vision, the butterfly's eyesight is sensitive to movement and color. The swallowtail butterflies, for example, regularly visit red flowers. Butterflies can also detect ultraviolet light, invisible to humans, suggesting that they may see colors in a way different to humans.

The middle zone of the butterfly body, the thorax, is divided into three segments, each supporting a pair of legs. Each leg has a jointed foot which ends in a pair of claws, permitting the butterfly to use its legs to walk or to cling. In one butterfly family, the Nymphalidae, the front legs are very short and held tucked into the body, giving the insects an unusual four-legged appearance. The forelegs on some spe-

This closeup of a Zebra Swallowtail (*Eurytides maracellus*) clearly shows its feeding tube coiled beneath its head. (James H. Carmichael, Jr.)

A freshly emerged Nivalis Copper (*Epidemia nivalis*) has delicately colored scales of lavender, pink, and gold. (R.J. Erwin)

cies are armed with hairy brushes, which are used to clean the antennae.

Two pairs of wings are connected to the second and third segments of the thorax. The pattern formed by the network of hollow veins sandwiched between the two thin membranes of each wing—called wing venation—is often a distinguishing feature of a species.

Butterflies and moths are unique among insects in

Phoebis butterflies gather at sundown to drink from a wet riverbank. (Frans Lanting)

that all three regions of the body—from their feet to their wing tips—are covered with thousands of delicate scales. These rows of overlapping scales, which to the naked eye look like colored powder, give the body its soft, downy appearance, as well as vivid coloring to the wings. Pigments in each scale create the color. In some species, microscopic ridges on the surface of each scale break up the light falling on them to produce shimmering metallic colors. The colors and patterns on the upper and under surfaces of the wings are often markedly different.

Among the scales of the male butterfly are specialized scent scales that produce pheromones. These scent scales may be distributed over the upper surface of the wing or collected in special patches on the veins.

Most of the butterfly's digestive system is in its abdomen, which is much softer than the head and thorax and consists of ten rings, or segments. Also located in the abdomen is the "fat body," which sustains the butterfly during long migratory flights and, in the female, nourishes eggs.

In the female, the end segment contains a special opening which receives the sperm from the male. Telescoped inside the opening is an egg-laying tube. The female produces her sex-attractant scent from glands located in the tip of the abdomen.

The end segments in the male contain a pair of claspers which grip the female during mating and surround the central ejaculatory organ. Inside are a pair of testes, fused into a single gland, that produce sperm. The presence or absence of the claspers indicates the sex of a butterfly.

The male and female of some species also look dramatically different, a condition known as sexual dimorphism. The Gorgon Copper (*Gaeides gorgon*),

16

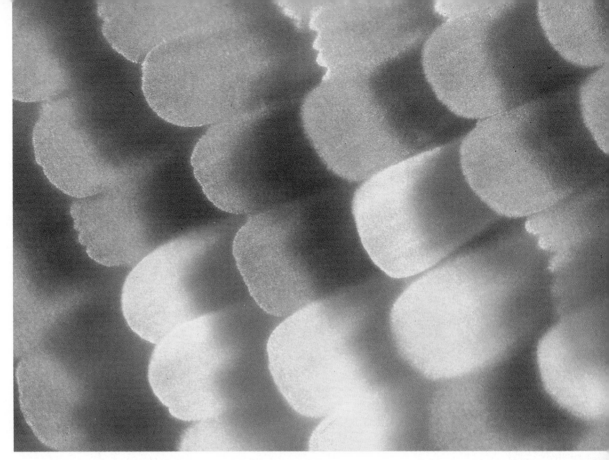

The golden wing scales
of a Gulf Fritillary
(*Agraulis vanillae*).
(Gary Retherford)

and the Mimic *(Hypolimnas misippus)* are examples of males and females with radically different markings.

Rarely, a butterfly will have the external characteristics of both male and female, a condition called gynandromorphism. This can be difficult to spot when both sexes look alike, but in such species as the Mimic, with pronounced sexual differences, they look very odd indeed. The wings on one side belong to one sex, while those on the opposite side belong to the other.

RANGE AND ENVIRONMENT

Like bees, as they fly from one flower to another, butterflies may help pollinate plants. Each species is very particular about its choice of plants. Butterflies are also particular about the climate and habitat in which they live. These idiosyncrasies limit both their distribution and range. Consequently, some species are found in only one small locality, one small part of a forest or one mountain valley. In Washington State, for example, the Nivalis Copper flies in the Eastern Cascades, but is never seen on the western slope of this range.

On the other hand, some species of butterfly are so adaptable that they populate almost every continent. The species which are good at migrating can use various habitats temporarily, thus extending their range by moving from place to place as the weather changes.

Some butterfly species produce several broods each year, although those living in harsher climates, with short summers and long winters, usually produce only one brood annually.

17

The male, left, and the female, right, of the Mimic *(Hypolimnas misippus)* species have radically different markings, a condition known as sexual dimorphism. (Joe B. Blossom)

CLIMATE AND HABITAT

Temperate Zone Butterflies

Butterflies can and do live everywhere—from the waterless desert to the highest, coldest mountaintop. In temperate regions—marked by cold winters and hot summers—species whose caterpillars feed on grasses are found in meadows, along the edges of woodlands and rivers, and in areas where forests have been cleared. The Pearly Crescentspot *(Phyciodes tharos)*, one of the most common meadow butterflies, showing the spots on the upper surface of its wings, glides over grasses, stopping to sip nectar from asters and the flowers of thistles.

The Great Spangled Fritillary *(Speyeria cybele)*, a large, tawny butterfly found in temperate climates, can be seen in the meadows and open woodlands of the East and, less commonly, in the moist pine and oak woods of the West. The adult female, with her sensitive "nose" for fragrances, lays eggs under bushes where violets have long since withered, but will reappear the next year, for her caterpillars will feed only on violets.

Many species are found in a temperate mixed woodland habitat, some flying low in shady woodland clearings, others skimming forest treetops. The California Dogface *(Zerene eurydice)*, California's spectacular state insect, flies in the foothills and open oak-covered slopes of the coastal ranges of

The female Great Spangled Fritillary *(Speyeria cybele)*, basking
on butterfly weed, above, will lay her eggs
beneath withered violets. (John Bova)

northern California all the way to Baja and western
Arizona.

Edwards' Hairstreak *(Satyrium edwardsii)* thrives in
open woods and sandy barrens. And the Acadian
Hairstreak *(Satyrium acadica)* can be found in damp
meadows near streams as well as in canyons near
willows.

Even the driest deserts have their butterfly populations, often species with limited range and distribution. Desert flowers found in the Mojave of
southeastern California, southern Nevada, and western Arizona support several species of butterfly, including the California Patch *(Chlosyne californica)*
and the Desert Green Hairstreak *(Callophrys comstocki)*. In years of ample rainfall the Desert Green

Hairstreak can be quite common among the desert
canyons and washes.

Mountain and Arctic Butterflies

In the high mountains and barren Arctic tundra,
short summers and bitterly cold nights make life
hard for fragile butterflies. To survive at all in such
hard climates butterflies must adapt themselves.

Species that are normally light-colored become
darker so that their wings can more readily absorb
the morning's first rays of sun and rapidly warm up
after a long, cold night. Some mountain butterflies
have developed long, feathery scales to help them
retain heat. Many high-mountain species lay their

eggs in the protective crevices of rocks rather than on plants. To avoid being blown away by strong winds, mountain butterflies fly in short spurts and rest in between by flattening themselves against rocks.

Mountain butterflies are attracted to wild flowers that bloom and flourish in high alpine meadows where few people go. The Palaeno Sulphur (*Colias palaeno*) can be found here, feeding on wild blueberries. These sulphurs sometimes reach as high as the Arctic Circle, as well as the Canadian subarctic. For many years, Arctic butterfly watchers have visited Churchill, Manitoba, a port on Hudson Bay, to see this northern sulphur.

The Dorcas Copper (*Epidemia dorcas*), one of the most prolific North American butterflies, thrives in the cooler environments of the North and the East, visiting meadows and forest clearings from Alaska east to Newfoundland and south to Maine and Minnesota. This butterfly is also found throughout the Rocky Mountains.

Tropical and Subtropical Butterflies

The largest, most dazzling butterflies are found in the warm regions of the earth near the equator. The range of color and pattern of tropical butterflies is remarkable, although the purpose of their fabulous dress is a mystery. It may be that in the vivid tropical jungles, where dark shadows are suddenly lit by bright patches of sun, a jeweled butterfly will more easily blend in.

In North America, warmth-loving butterflies are limited mostly to Mexico and southern Florida, although some Mexican species, such as the Pavon (*Doxocopa pavon*) and the Blue Wing (*Myscelia ethusa*), stray over the Texas border each year, giving U.S. observers a glimpse of their bright wings.

In southern Florida, the West Indian Buckeye (*Junonia evarete*) mingles with the Buckeye (*Junonia coenia*), and the two species are often confused.

The White Peacock (*Anartia jatrophae*), mostly limited to the tropics, occasionally invades the North,

sometimes straying as far as Massachusetts. Similarly, the Malachite (*Siproeta stelenes*), sometimes seen in Florida, may be a stray from Mexico.

HIBERNATION

The complete life cycle of a butterfly—from egg to imago to death—may last one brief summer or, in some cases, a year or longer. Some butterflies are able to survive harsh climatic conditions by entering periods of hibernation, or diapause. In temperate climates, diapause is triggered by winter; in the tropics, by a dry season.

The stage of life at which the insect hibernates varies in different species and, within the same species, in different parts of its geographic range. Eggs, caterpillars, chrysalises, and occasionally even adult butterflies may enter diapause. Once such a period is entered a certain amount of time must elapse—like the timer on a safe—before active life is resumed. This is to ensure that the insect does not emerge too early during a favorable spell in otherwise harsh conditions.

In temperate regions, where hot summers give way to freezing winters, the winter is often passed in the chrysalis stage. Only a few adult butterflies are capable of hibernating, or overwintering. The Compton Tortoiseshell (*Nymphalis vau-album*) and Milbert's Tortoiseshell (*Aglais milberti*) are among the species that may overwinter as adults. The butterfly finds a sheltered spot in a cave, under leaves, or even inside a house; while hibernating its body functions slow down so much that it does not need to feed.

SELF-PROTECTION

Butterflies are the most flamboyant of creatures, and human observers attribute a multitude of purposes to their distinctive markings. Startling colors and patterns may remind predators that a particular butterfly is poisonous and should be avoided; bright col-

A greenish-yellow Sulphur blends with leaves for near-perfect camouflage. (J.H. Robinson)

ors may also imitate a dangerous insect or attract a mate.

In the case of the Ruddy Daggerwing (*Marpesia petreus*), a large, bright butterfly that seems to invite attention by displaying the long, dashing tails of its hind wings, the tails may actually serve to distract the predators from the butterfly's vulnerable body or main wings. Some butterflies take on the patterns and colors of their environment to hide from their enemies. The greenish-yellow sulphurs, for example, often mimic leaves.

Many butterflies have a drab pattern on the undersurface of their wings. When the butterfly is at rest with its wings folded, the undersurface is exposed, harmonizing with leaves, bark, or rocks. Disturbed, the butterfly flashes its wings and the bright upper surface startles a predator.

When resting on a tree trunk or branch, the dark, ragged underwings of the Mourning Cloak (*Nymphalis antiopa*) are perfectly camouflaged against bark. At the approach of a predator, it makes a "clicking" sound and flaps instantly into flight, showing creamy yellow margins and brilliant blue spots all along the edges of its upper surface. This spectacular butterfly can be found in virtually every corner of North America.

The Comma (*Polygonia comma*), named for a distinguishing mark on the undersides of its hind wings, retreats when threatened; it hangs upside down from a twig, its irregular outline giving a perfect imitation of a dead leaf.

Ragged wing borders and mottled undersides help the Question Mark (*Polygonia interrogationis*) to hide itself in woodland glades from Canada to Mexico. No other anglewing has such distinct tails trailing from the hind wings, stamped with the silvery

21

At rest on a branch, the Mourning Cloak (*Nymphalis antiopa*) is almost invisible. (John Serrao)

When the Mourning Cloak flaps its wings the colorfully patterned upper surfaces flash. (Kjell B. Sandved)

comma and offset dot that form a question mark.

A few species of butterflies employ a unique protective trick called mimicry to deceive predators. Mimicry usually takes the form of a good-tasting species copying the color and pattern of a species with an unpleasant smell or taste. Birds learn to recognize the warning patterns of the harmful species and leave it—and its look-alikes—alone. In each stage of its life, the innocent Viceroy (*Basilarchia archippus*) takes on a deceptive appearance. For example, as a chrysalis, it looks like a bird dropping; as an adult, it mimics the poisonous Monarch. The southern population of the Viceroy mimics the chestnut-colored, poisonous Queen (*Danaus gilippus*).

MIGRATION

The movement of whole populations of butterflies is a spectacular example of insect migration. These mass flights are usually in one direction only—from the place where the butterflies were born to a new area.

There are several possible reasons for these one-way passages: to avoid overpopulation; to find a new home when a habitat is destroyed; or in response to the changing seasons. Butterflies are often on the move when the weather improves, moving north as new plant growth becomes available for egg laying. Along the way, butterflies may stop to rest, mate, and lay eggs.

The Painted Lady (*Vanessa cardui*) is one of the world's great travelers, found throughout Africa, Europe, and Asia, as well as in North America. These butterflies are found year-round in the southern deserts. In February and March, as spring breaks, the Painted Lady begins infiltrating the North and the East once again, the number of immigrants fluctuating from year to year. By late spring, they inhabit

The ragged shape of its wings helps camouflage the Comma (*Polygonia comma*); its distinguishing silver mark is visible on the underwing. (J.A. Hancock)

Beginning in late summer, millions of Monarch butterflies (*Danaus plexippus*) take flight on a long migration to winter in California and Mexico. (Francois Gohier)

the whole continent. When the hard frosts come in the North, the Painted Lady is killed off by the cold.

Similarly, the Cloudless Giant Sulphur (*Phoebis sennae*) migrates in summer to areas far north of its winter range in Mexico and the southern United States. Summer may find millions of these butterflies in relatively small areas, occasionally appearing in the Rocky Mountains or New York State. All of these northern immigrants die at summer's end.

The famous Monarch (*Danaus plexippus*) breaks most of the rules of butterfly migration. Beginning in late summer, this gorgeous, familiar butterfly flies north to south, from Canada and the eastern seaboard, across the United States to its winter quarters in California and Mexico. At the places where the Monarch stops along the way to rest, the trees are covered with these large butterflies, whose wingspan may reach up to 4 inches. Having survived the winter, the butterflies then begin to fly back north in the spring. They usually go only part of the way, then stop, lay eggs on milkweeds, and die. It is their descendants that finish the return trip, although a few older butterflies, distinguished by their worn and ragged wings, may be found among the returning brood.

The Buckeye (*Junonia coenia*), with their lovely scalloped wings and bright eyespots, sometimes rival the Monarch in their spectacular autumn migrations south along the east coast, but their journeys are only one way.

To a great extent, migrating butterflies travel where the wind carries them, but some are strong, high flyers able to maintain their own direction against buffeting wind currents. The fastest known butterfly is the Monarch, which can keep up with a car traveling at speeds between 45 and 65 miles per hour. Mark and recapture experiments have proved that the Monarch can cover more than 3,000 miles in only a few days.

ENDANGERED SPECIES

As their habitats have been increasingly destroyed, the butterfly population has begun to disappear from grasslands and forests, as well as from urban and suburban areas. Their fading presence touches each of us in ways that we can barely articulate. In every language, in every corner of the world, the butterfly is the spirit of beauty and unending summer.

In the past, butterfly species were often depleted by avid collectors. Many countries now have laws preventing excessive collecting, and in recent years fewer species have been destroyed by collectors. Today, butterfly admirers tend to breed butterflies rather than kill them, photograph them rather than mount them. The threat to survival now comes from the destruction of their habitat. Dependent as butterflies are on wild plants and open countryside, they are extremely vulnerable to changes in the environment, especially those caused by human beings. Throughout the world, even in the tropics where butterflies thrive, such important habitats as the tropical rain forests are being lost. Many harmless butterflies are also killed by herbicides and insecticides. In recent times, many of the most beautiful species have become first rare, then endangered, then extinct.

The Regal Fritillary (*Speyeria idalia*) occurs in a number of states, but as its natural grassland habitat is plowed up, this butterfly has become increasingly rare.

The Bluish Green Hairstreak (*Callophrys viridis*) used to thrive on islands, hills, and shoreline around the San Francisco Bay Area. Today almost all populations have been eliminated as the result of urbanization.

And the famous Xerces Blue (*Blaucopsyche xerces*), which once thrived in the coastal sand dunes of the San Francisco Peninsula, is now extinct. The Xerces Society, a worldwide conservation group, was formed in memory of the California Xerces Blue, last collected on March 23, 1943.

A NOTE ABOUT NOMENCLATURE

The scientific name of each animal consists of two Latin or latinized words: the first is the name of the genus to which the animal is assigned; the second is the name of the species. Often these names are mythological—Phoebus, Danaus, Aphrodite. Or they sometimes refer to the extraordinary beauty of the butterfly, or some special physical or behavioral characteristic. A butterfly may be named for the first person who identified it, such as *Oarisma edwardsii*, named for Willian Henry Edwards, a nineteenth-century collector and author.

These Latin names are retained all over the world. By contrast, the colloquial or common name by which a butterfly is known often changes from country to country.

Each butterfly is categorized in ascending order, beginning with its species, for certain identification is known only by species. (A butterfly belongs to a certain species because it can breed only with other members of that species.) All higher divisions are artificial. The boundaries between one genus and another, between families, or even between phyla are blurred, and are largely a matter of convenience and convention.

While the seven hundred North American species are grouped into nine families (some scientists divide them into ten) this classification is controversial. Any arrangement to sort out the profusion of names and revisions in scientific nomenclature that have occurred over decades of scientific study is necessarily a compromise. In this book, the traditional family divisions and names are retained. Examples of each of the nine families found in North America, have been selected for their rarity, unusual behavior, and, sometimes, for their abundance.

A note amid confusion: In the animal kingdom, all superfamily names end in "-oidea," family names end in "-idae," and subfamily names end in "-inae."

The Buckeye *(Junonia coenia)*. (Kjell B. Sandved)

PAPILIONIDAE
SWALLOWTAILS AND PARNASSIANS

The Eastern Black
Swallowtail
(*Papilio polyxenes*).

The famous family Papilionidae ranges from the pale, mountain-dwelling parnassians to the brilliant Australasian birdwing *(Ornithoptera)*, the world's largest butterfly. These large, powerful fliers are among the most splendid of all butterflies. Some females have wing spans of 5½ inches or more. At the other end of the scale are the tiny dragontail butterflies *(Lamproptera)* from India and Malaysia, whose wings, tip to tip, measure less than 2 inches.

The unusual shapes and vivacious coloring of many Papilionidae attract the attention of lepidopterists everywhere. Consequently, they have been observed more carefully than many other butterfly families. More than seven hundred species are distributed throughout the world, but fewer than thirty species are found in North America. All North American members of the Papilionidae family are swallowtails or parnassians.

SWALLOWTAILS

Swallowtails are easily recognized by their large bright wings and long tails. All swallowtails have patterns of contrasting colors—yellow and black, white and black, or blue and black. Often their wings also bear conspicuous orange and blue spots.

Their eggs are somewhat spherical, and their smooth-skinned caterpillars usually have large eyespots. The swallowtail caterpillar possesses a unique structure called an osmeterium, a brightly colored forked organ behind the head, which it can erect. When the caterpillar is disturbed, it rears up in a

27

threatening manner and thrusts out this gland, which emits a foul smell.

The angular chrysalis resembles bits of leaf or wood; it hangs upright throughout winter, held by a silken girdle.

In North America most swallowtails fall into four general subgroups: Black *(Papilio)*, Giant *(Heraclides)*, Tiger *(Pterourus)*, and Pipevine *(Battus)*.

BLACK SWALLOWTAILS (Papilio)

Black swallowtails are black with yellow spots that may become broad bands.

EASTERN BLACK SWALLOWTAIL
(Papilio polyxenes)

On its upper wing surfaces the Eastern Black Swallowtail is black to blue-black, with a blue cloud on the edges of the hind wing. A bright orange eyespot with a black pupil marks the inner corner of the hind wing. Rows of yellow spots and chevrons flash on both sides of the wings.

The Eastern Black Swallowtail can be found from the Canadian Rockies south to Arizona and Mexico, all the way east to the Atlantic. These butterflies like gardens and open farmland, meadows and riverbanks. They flit and stall among parsley or carrot plants and sip nectar from phlox and milkweed.

The Eastern and Western Black Swallowtail sometimes fly together in the Rocky Mountains, but the Eastern Black can better tolerate suburban habitats.

OLD WORLD SWALLOWTAIL
(Papilio machaon)

Yellow spots along the outer margins, with a band of shiny blue spots across the hind wing mark the Old World Swallowtail. A broad band of dull yellow spots fills the middle of the wings. A distinguishing orange eyespot with a black rim is on the hind wing. The undersurfaces of the wings are a paler version of the same pattern.

The Old World Swallowtail, sometimes called the Alaskan Swallowtail, flies in relatively inaccessible areas of North America, through the forest edges in the mountains and alpine tundra around the Arctic Ocean in Alaska, east across the Yukon and Northwest Territories, and southeast across Canada to the northern shores of Lake Superior. This butterfly is so seldom observed that the life cycle for North American populations is as yet unknown. The host plant in Alaska is believed to be arctic sagebrush.

ANISE SWALLOWTAIL *(Papilio zelicaon)*

The dramatically patterned Anise Swallowtail is more yellow than black. Both surfaces of its wings are filled with large lemon-yellow spots. The hind wing is flushed with blue, and the inside corners show two orange eyespots with large, round pupils. The Anise Swallowtail has yellow side stripes along its black abdomen. Like the Eastern Black, the Anise Swallowtail is among the most adaptable of North American butterflies. It can be found everywhere west of the Rockies, flying from beaches to mountaintops, from city lots to deserts and canyons. The only habitat it avoids are dense, dark forests.

GIANT SWALLOWTAILS (Heraclides)

Giant swallowtails are extremely large, brown and yellow butterflies with wingspreads up to 5½ inches. In fact, the Giant Swallowtail *(Heraclides cresphontes)* and a similar species, the Thoas Swallowtail *(Heraclides thoas)*, along with the female Tiger Swallowtail *(Pterourus glaucus)*, are the largest North American butterflies. Mottled olive or brown and buff-colored, the citrus-loving caterpillars often resemble large bird droppings.

The long, spoon-shaped tails with their yellow dots give the Giant Swallowtail *(Heraclides cresphontes)* a unique look. The butterfly's abdomen is yellow, and it has a black line down its back. On top, the surface of the wings is almost black, with two broad bands of yellow spots that meet at the wing tips.

The Old World Swallowtail (*Papilio machaon*), sometimes called the Alaskan Swallowtail, is rarely seen. (Kjell B. Sandved)

The Giant Swallowtail (*Heraclides cresphontes*), one of the largest North American butterflies, has long, spoon-shaped tails and a yellow abdomen. (Ray Coleman)

The Tiger Swallowtail (*Pterourus glaucus*) is one of several species of yellow and black Tigers found in North America. (Kjell B. Sandved)

There is a blue and an orange spot at the corner of each hind wing. Underneath, the wings are distinctly different, almost solid yellow with black veins and borders.

Citrus growers call the Giant Swallowtail "Orange Dog" and often spray it to death to prevent its caterpillars from consuming crops. In the South, the Giant Swallowtail lives year-round in multiple broods, farther north only in autumn and summer broods. The Giant Swallowtail likes sunny, open areas and citrus groves from southern Canada through the United States all the way to Mexico.

TIGER SWALLOWTAILS (Pterourus)

Tiger swallowtails are generally yellow with black stripes. They survive on a wide variety of plants, and cover a vast range. Several species of tigers live in North America, but the most widely distributed is the Tiger Swallowtail (*Pterourus glaucus*). Some of the females are black. Their coloring lets them mimic the distasteful Pipevine Swallowtail, which has helped to make this one of the more abundant species.

Another magnificent species of tiger is the Spicebush (*Pterourus troilus*), which also mimics the Pipevine Swallowtail, but both males and females have two arcs of bright orange dots on the undersurface of the hind wings.

PIPEVINE SWALLOWTAILS (Battus)

Named for their caterpillar's host plant, the pipevine, these gorgeous black butterflies are found throughout North America. Although the adults of this species favor honeysuckle, orchids, and lilacs, the distasteful pipevine favored by the caterpillars give these butterflies a bad reputation among birds. Several other species of swallowtails have evolved to resemble pipevine swallowtails, which gives them equal protection from predators.

ZEBRA SWALLOWTAIL
(Eurytides marcellus)

A few species of swallowtails fit into none of the other groups. The black-and-white striped Zebra Swallowtail, for example, with its long, triangular wings and swordlike tail, looks like a tiny kite. The Zebra Swallowtail is found throughout the Atlantic seaboard, west to the Great Plains. Although the Zebra Swallowtail thrives in a wide variety of habitats, from woodlands to meadows and riverbanks, this butterfly cannot survive in suburban development.

PARNASSIANS

The parnassians or apollos (Parnassius) are quite different from other members of the family Papilionidae. Their bodies are densely clothed with hair and their wings are rounded and nearly transparent. The see-through wings, white or yellowish with black checks and red spots, may span up to 3 inches.

Parnassians dwell in the mountains of the Northwest where they are among the most familiar alpine butterflies. Unlike other members of this family, the parnassians are relatively slow and lazy fliers. All females have a waxy gray or black pouch at the tip of the abdomen.

CLODIUS PARNASSIAN
(Parnassius clodius)

The milky-white Clodius Parnassian, with its black

Another species of Tiger is the Spicebush (Pterourus troilus). The female Spicebush is black, which allows it to mimic the poisonous Pipevine Swallowtails. (Michael Lustbader)

checks and red spots, is found only in North America. The Clodius flies slowly along forest edges and in the cool mountains and shaded canyons of the Northwest, from Alaska south to California, and east to Wyoming and Utah. These butterflies have disappeared from the Snake River Canyon in Idaho, where they once flew in abundance.

PHOEBUS PARNASSIAN
(Parnassius phoebus)

The Phoebus Parnassian sometimes flies in the same mountains as the Clodius, but usually at higher altitudes. Its antennae are banded in black and white. (Clodius antennae are all black). The wings of the males are cream to snow white, with black and gray markings and red spots above and below. On the outer edge of the forewings there are black spots. The females are duskier, with more black and gray markings.

The life cycle of the Phoebus Parnassian may last two years. Its eggs hatch in summer. The yellow-spotted black caterpillars overwinter, then pupate in smooth, tan chrysalises wrapped in cocoons that are scattered in the grass or among debris.

The Phoebus is famous as a cold-weather flyer. (It has even been known to fly through snow.) The higher and colder the region, the more numerous the butterfly's dark scales, allowing it to quickly absorb the limited warmth from the sun.

The Clodius Parnassian (Parnassius clodius), right. (Kjell B. Sandved)

The Phoebus Parnassian (Parnassius phoebus), below, is a high-mountain, cold-weather flier. (J.L. Lepore)

PIERIDAE
WHITES AND ORANGETIPS
BRIMSTONES AND SULPHURS

The Great Southern White (*Ascia monuste*). (Ken Brate)

The Pieridae are among the most abundant butterflies in all regions of the United States, although of the approximately one thousand species worldwide, there are only fifty-five to sixty species in North America.

Most pierids are some shade of white, yellow, or yellowish-green, but the wings of some species are marbled and a few, like the Sara Orangetip (*Anthocharis sara*), seem to have dipped their wings in bright orange paint. The color of a particular species may change from season to season and the male and female also may display different colors.

The eggs of Pieridae are characteristically spindle-shaped, and the green caterpillars are smooth and cylindrical. For the most part the caterpillars of whites prefer plants of the cabbage family (crucifers), and those of the sulphurs prefer legumes, although pierids overall may feed on a fairly wide variety of plants.

The cone-shaped chrysalis forms upright, supported by a silken girdle. The butterfly may pupate through the winter and emerge in the spring.

North American species of Pieridae are usually medium-sized with wingspans between 1 1/4 and 2 inches, although there are also some very tiny and some giant sulphurs. Several of the species migrate in hordes, which accounts for their extensive distri-

The familiar and prolific Cabbage White (*Artogeis rapae*). (Stephen Dalton)

35

The Sara Orangetip (*Anthocharis sara*). (Kjell B. Sandved)

bution. Tropical species that emigrate northward in spring are unable to withstand the winter and die out with the cold.

WHITES AND ORANGETIPS (Pieriniae)

These are some of the most familiar of all butterflies. White butterflies often have wings with black borders or black-and-white checks or forewings tipped with orange. The marblewings have greenish-yellow marbling on the undersurface of the wings.

CABBAGE WHITE OR "SMALL WHITE" (*Artogeia rapae*)

The Cabbage White is perhaps the most prolific and successful of all butterfly species. This familiar butterfly has wings of milky white above with charcoal wing tips; the undersurface is usually pale yellow with grayish specks. This native of Eurasia was inadvertently introduced to North America through

Quebec in 1860, and since then has wandered throughout the United States. All habitats—cities and farms, hills and gardens, plains and fields—are the same to the Small White. Farmers and gardeners consider the Cabbage White caterpillar a pest because of its zestful appetite for cabbages and other crucifers.

GREAT SOUTHERN WHITE
(Ascia monuste)

With its full, draping wings, bordered with dark scallops, the Great Southern White is a butterfly in full formal dress. Common throughout the southern United States, this species builds up to huge numbers, and then, as the food supply diminishes, travels north in erratic mass migrations. These spontaneous one-way flights are most likely the result of explosions of butterfly populations, causing large numbers of their species to seek greener pastures. The migrating butterflies are usually darker, and the wings of

the female may be entirely suffused with smoky-brown or gray scales.

SARA ORANGETIP (Anthocharis sara)

Sara Orangetip, with its bright orange wing tips on top and marbled undersides, is nearly as successful as the Cabbage White in its ability to exploit diverse habitats. However, it usually has only spring and summer generations because the caterpillars eat only flowers and seed pods. In the far West, the Sara Orangetip flies over deserts and up mountain slopes. A Rocky Mountain population flies in the cool woods and meadows of the high mountains.

BRIMSTONES AND SULPHURS
(Coliadinae)

As their names imply, these are mostly yellow butterflies. They are found all over the world, and some species are intrepid migrants.

The Common Sulphur or "Clouded Sulphur" (Colias philodice) is found all over the United States, except in tropical Florida. (Charles Mann)

The Orange Sulphur or "Alfalfa Butterfly" (*Colias eurytheme*)
sports a pink fringe. (Richard Parker)

Sulphurs range in hue from pale yellowish-white to bright yellow, orange, and yellowish-green. Several have black borders above. Others show delicate pink fringes and pink-rimmed spots below. Many sulphurs are common in meadows and parks, but a few species fly only in cold, high mountains.

COMMON SULPHUR OR "CLOUDED SULPHUR" (*Colias philodice*)

The Common Sulphur, which feeds on clover, alfalfa, and many other legumes, occupies all corners of the United States, except for Florida. It prefers the open country and is seldom seen in dense forests or extreme deserts.

The adult butterfly lays a single chartreuse egg on a clover leaf. From this egg a bright green caterpillar emerges. The green chrysalis overwinters.

ORANGE SULPHUR OR "ALFALFA BUTTERFLY" (*Colias eurytheme*)

The upper wing surface of the Orange Sulphur is bright orange with a pink tint and wide, black borders. Below, the wings are solid yellow, orange, or greenish-yellow, distinguished by one or two big silver spots and a row of smaller brown spots. The wings of the Orange Sulphur are edged with a pink fringe.

Like the Common Sulphur, the Orange thrives in nearly any open space, particularly alfalfa fields. Because of this food preference, the Orange and the Common Sulphurs often colonize the same area. In the normal course of events, the two species do not merge. But when they are superabundant, they often hybridize and produce butterflies in varying shades of yellow or orange.

The large White-angled Sulphur (*Anteos clorinde*) shows its distinctive yellow bars and red spots. (Kjell B. Sandved)

The large, powerful wings of the Orange-barred Giant Sulphur (*Phoebis philea*) make it a strong flier. (Kjell B. Sandved)

WHITE ANGLED SULPHUR
(Anteos clorinde)

The large, angled wings of this species, which sometimes reach 3½ inches across, guarantee that it resembles no other butterfly. It is all white above, with a distinctive red spot on each wing, splashed with a bright yellow bar across the forewing. Underneath, the wings are jade green. In late summer, this robust resident of southern Texas occasionally strays into Arizona, New Mexico, and Colorado.

ORANGE-BARRED GIANT SULPHUR
(Phoebis philea)

This is another very large butterfly, whose wings measure up to 3¼ inches. The male is yellow, with a broad, orange bar crossing the forewing and bordering the hind wing. The bars are less distinct on the female. The underwings are a blend of pink, lavender, and orange, with black spots on each wing.

The Orange-barred Giant Sulphur is a New World tropical butterfly found in southern Florida and southern Texas, occasionally straying as far north as Nebraska and New York. It is capable of strong, powerful flights, but tends to stop frequently to feed, which makes it fairly easy to observe within its range.

CALIFORNIA DOGFACE OR "FLYING PANSY" (Zerene eurydice)

Eurydice flies from California's coastal ranges and lower western Sierras into western Arizona. In the San Bernardino Mountains it may overlap with the Dogface Butterfly *(Zerene cesonia)* and the two species may hybridize.

The upper surface of the forewings of the Dogface Butterfly are yellow with thick, black margins indented in a poodle-head pattern. In the California Dogface, only the male has the distinctive dogface markings. It is more orange all over, with a purple or plum-red sheen on its forewings.

The famous California Dogface or "Flying Pansy" *(Colias eurydice)*. (Kjell B. Sandved)

LYCAENIDAE
GOSSAMER WINGS

The Colorado Hairstreak
(Hypaurotis crysalus).
(Kjell B. Sandved)

Of the seven thousand species of Lycaenidae world-wide, only a hundred live in North America. These are small butterflies, with a maximum wingspan of 2 inches.

Most species have metallic coloring on their upper wing surfaces, usually shades of blue, green, purple, or copper. The undersides are typically spotted or streaked in intricate patterns.

Their coloring derives from two different types of scales—pigmented scales and light-refracting scales.

A distinguishing feature of this family are the delicately ringed antennae.

In most species, the males have shortened forelegs held close to the body, and only the four hind legs can be used for walking. In the females all six legs are well developed.

This family Lycaenidae includes four groups or subfamilies: blues (Polyommatinae), coppers (Lycaeniae), hairstreaks (Theclinae), and the Harvester (*Feniseca tarquinius*).

While their color names identify them to some extent—blues tend to be blue and coppers are mostly copper-colored—there are many color variations. Similarly, hairstreaks usually have tailed wings, but some species are tailless. The females of some species, especially the blues, may be dark brown and inconspicuous.

The eggs of the Lycaenidae are a flattened disc shape or domed and are delicately ribbed or furrowed. The green or brown caterpillars tend to be flat and tapered at the ends.

The caterpillars feed on many kinds of plants,

The Harvester (*Feniseca tarquinius*) is the only carnivorous butterfly in North America. (Rod Planck)

consuming buds, flowers, and fruit. An exception is the Harvester, a carnivore which preys upon aphids, making these caterpillars a great asset to gardeners and growers.

Caterpillars of many blues and hairstreaks have honey glands that attract ants. The ants milk the gland of small drops of sweet fluid. In turn, the ants protect the caterpillars from parasites that might damage them. Thus, both insects thrive and live together harmoniously.

The chrysalises of the Lycaenidae are short and compact. They are usually attached by a silk girdle to the leaves of the host plant, or they may lie loose among ground litter. Some resemble bird droppings. The chrysalis of the Harvester looks like a tiny monkey's head.

The chrysalis of most butterflies is as still and as silent as a grave. But the chrysalis of the Lycaenidae occasionally emits a faint crackling sound, which lepidopterists believe may help protect the overwintering pupa from attack by small predators.

THE HARVESTER (*Feniseca tarquinius*)

There are several tropical species of carnivorous gossamer wings, but in North America only the Harvester is present. The adult butterflies feed off the sweet excretions, or honeydew, of aphids, destroying the pests in the process and inadvertently protecting crops. The Harvesters are rather languid as adults, quite different in flight from other, quicker butterflies. They fly slowly and often stop to bask in the sun.

HAIRSTREAKS (Theclinae)

Hairstreaks are named for the delicate lines traced on the undersides of the wings. Although represented in all regions, this subfamily peaks in tropical America where some species rank among the most exquisite of all butterflies.

Most hairstreaks have thin, hairlike tails projecting from the hind wings and delicate streaks on the undersurface. Each hind wing may also bear a burst of bright red, orange, or blue below. Some hairstreaks, however, lack tails and have only faint markings on their undersides.

COLORADO HAIRSTREAK
(Hypaurotis crysalus)

This brilliant, deep purple hairstreak with dark margins on the outer edges of its wings is one of North America's most exotic-looking butterflies. In contrast to the richly colored upper surfaces, the undersides of its wings are light brownish-gray with white-edged lines and a short orange band; on each hind wing near the tail is a blue patch with a black-centered orange spot.

Although its names suggests it is found only in Colorado, in fact *Hypaurotis crysalus* flies the oak canyons and mountain foothills through much of the Southwest, from Utah south through eastern Nevada and Colorado all the way to southeastern Arizona and New Mexico.

Unlike most sun-loving butterflies, the Colorado Hairstreak will fly on cloudy days and may even fly in the rain.

RED-BANDED HAIRSTREAK
(Calycopis cecrops)

Like most hairstreaks, it is the underwing surfaces that distinctively mark *Calycopis cecrops.* On top, the butterfly is brown-black, with pale iridescent blue patches on the hind wings near the tails. But underneath this hairstreak shows a bright, jagged swath of white and black, the inner edge painted with a broad, flame-red band. Between the tails on the hind wing is a large, black spot. Overall, the butterfly usually measures under 1 inch.

The showy caterpillar of the Red-banded Hairstreak has a thick, brown, hairy coat with a greenish stripe down its back. Its host plants are the dwarf sumar, croton, and wax myrtle. The adult butterfly favors nectar from the flowers of these host plants.

The Red-banded Hairstreak, which is especially active at twilight, flies in the open countryside, along forest edges and barrens from Ohio and New Jersey south to Texas and Florida. It is especially common along the southeastern coast.

BROWN ELFIN (Incisalia augustinus)

Augustinus is the most common North American elfin, ranging from Canada south to California, New Mexico, Michigan, and Virginia.

Above, the Brown Elfin is warm-brown to grayish, and sometimes rust-colored. Below, the wings are a purplish light brown deepening to a dark brown toward the inner half. The wing margins are scalloped and usually checkered. The Brown Elfin measures up to 1 1/8 inches across.

The Brown Elfin's wide distribution probably results from the indiscriminate appetite of its caterpillars, which can thrive on a great array of plants, including blueberries, bearberry, and azaleas in the

East, and lilac, apples, and madrone in the West.

The Brown Elfin flies mostly in open glades and forest edges, but it is also found in the desert.

CORAL HAIRSTREAK (*Harkenclenus titus*)

The swiftly flying Coral Hairstreak stops frequently to dally at the flowers of its favorite nectar sources, the butterfly weed or, in the Rockies, the bee plant. This butterfly shows off its distinctive ringed antennae.

This hairstreak has no tails, and it is the only tailless hairstreak that also has a row of coral spots on its underwings.

Like other hairstreaks, the Red-banded Hairstreak (*Calycopis cecrops*), left, is known for its highly marked underwing surfaces and delicate tails. (Ken Brate)

Its downy, yellowish-green caterpillars feed on plums and wild cherries.

The Coral Hairstreak varies widely in coloring. The male has pointed wings and is usually dark brown above. The female has rounded wings and is usually light brown above. Sometimes the upper wing surfaces are flushed with orange. There is always a prominent row of large, bright coral spots along the entire hind wing margin underneath.

The Coral Hairstreak is found in brushy clearings and roadsides, wherever wild cherries and plums grow, from British Columbia to central California, northeastern Arizona, Texas, and Georgia. It is fairly common in the Northeast, and sometimes localized in the mountain canyons of the West.

The Brown Elfin (*Incisalia augustinus*), below, shows off the ringed antennae common to the family Lycaenidae. (Rod Planck)

The Coral Hairstreak (*Harkenclenus titus*) always has a row of large, bright coral spots underneath each hind wing. (L. West)

BLUES (Polyommatinae)

These small- to medium-sized butterflies are familiar in gardens and woods. Blues are found in all regions, but are less tropical than other Lycaenidae; in North America the mountains throng with blues. The pattern of the underside spotting is characteristic, but subject to enormous variation.

ACMON BLUE OR "EMERALD-STUDDED BLUE" (*Icaricia acmon*)

This bright, lilac-blue butterfly with its narrow, black margins is distinguished on its hind wings by an or-ange band, with an outermost row of black dots capped with shimmering green. As if that were not enough, this gorgeous butterfly has a white fringe all around the edges of its wings.

The Acmon Blue is found everywhere in the far West, and often flies and mingles with other blues. The Acmon Blue can always be distinguished when the sun catches the emerald green scales on the edge of its hind wings.

EASTERN TAILED BLUE (*Everes comyntas*)

Because the low-flying Eastern Tailed Blue can toler-ate human invasion of its habitat, it is one of the

East's most abundant butterflies. In fact, populations of this mainly eastern butterfly have settled west of the Rockies after people altered the landscape, probably because its favored host plants—clovers, beans, wild pea, and other legumes—thrive in such disturbed sites as road cuts, railroad lines, and crop fields.

The Eastern Tailed Blue is distinguished by its threadlike tail. The male is a bright silver-blue above, with narrow, dark margins and orange and black spots on its hind wings; the female is gray flushed with blue. Underneath, the wings are grayish white with distinct curved rows of gray and black spots. There are conspicuous orange blotches above the hind wing tail. The butterfly is edged with white fringe.

SILVERY BLUE (*Glaucopsyche lygdamus*)

Because it can withstand cold, windy weather the Silvery Blue is often the first butterfly to appear in spring, easily identified by the bold, crooked row of black dots, each ringed with white, on the gray undersurface of its wings. Above, the wings of the male are silver blue with narrow, black margins; the female has darker wings, with wider, more diffuse mar-

The row of black dots on the hind wing of the Acmon Blue (*Icaricia acmon*) are capped with shimmering green scales. (Kjell B. Sandved)

The Eastern Tailed Blue *(Everes comyntas)*, above, is distinguished by its threadlike tails and beautiful white fringe. The pale undersurfaces of its hind wings are marked with orange blotches, left. (Above: J.H. Robinson. Left: L. West)

The Silvery Blue (*Glaucopsyche lygdamus*), right, is identified by a bold, crooked row of black dots ringed with white on the undersurfaces of its wings. (Stephen P. Parker)

gins. Sometimes the female is almost totally brown above, with the merest trace of blue at the base of her wings.

Many separate races of Silvery Blue have been identified, from Alaska and Nova Scotia, south to Baja California, through the Southwest, Alabama, and Georgia. They are comfortable in almost every kind of habitat, from sea level to mountain meadows, and their caterpillars thrive on many different host plants, including deer weed, lupine, and wild pea. The coloring and iridescence of the Silvery Blue varies widely among these geographic populations. By late summer these cool blues have disappeared.

COPPERS (Lycaeninae)

These butterflies usually have bright orange markings or bands. Many have black spots on all wing surfaces. This third division of gossamer wings is smaller in number and more northerly in distribution than the other two groups. Coppers tend to be highly variable in coloring, all the way from a bright, brassy color to a dingy gray-brown. Because many species are flushed with violet over copper, and a few species are blue, observers may confuse them with the blues. The patterns on their underwings are also similar to those of the blues.

PURPLISH COPPER (*Epidemia helloides*)

Epidemia helloides is an example of a copper with strong purplish reflections. This butterfly, the most common copper in California, penetrates many parts of the Northwest that are almost devoid of butterflies. It flies from sea level to mountaintops in many different habitats. The Purplish Copper measures less than 1¼ inches, but it is much hardier than its small size would suggest.

The Purplish Copper *(Epidemia helloides)*. (Kjell B. Sandved)

RIODINIDA
METALMARKS

The Fatal Metalmark
(Calephelis nemesis).
(R. J. Erwin)

One of the largest butterfly families, with estimates between one thousand and two thousand species, the vast majority of metalmarks are found in Central and South America. Elsewhere in the world the metalmarks are seldom seen.

A number of species are native to North America, especially the Mormon metalmarks *(Apodemia mormo)* and several Calephelis. These North American metalmarks are quite small, ranging in wing span from 5/8 of an inch to 2 inches. Metalmarks usually hold their wings out flat, although some rest their wings at a 45-degree angle.

Little is known about this butterfly family because of the butterflies' secretive behavior. Many species are extremely localized, seldom venturing forth from their habitat. They may live in dense forests, resting under leaves like moths. Other species sometimes visit flowers or congregate in damp places. Some fly high among the treetops. The Swamp, Northern, and Little metalmarks cover most of the United States east of the Mississippi, but they never overlap. The Swamp Metalmark *(Calephelis muticum)* is found in more northern and wetter areas.

In wing shape, pattern, and coloring, metalmarks show a startling variation. Many tropical members of this family are vividly colored in magnificent patterns, some displaying brilliant metallic and iridescent shades. The wings may be rounded or angular, and in some cases extravagantly tailed. North American species tend to be more subtly colored with checkered patterns on the wings. Some metalmarks resemble moths. In this case, the brown, gray, or rust upper wings strongly contrast with the lower wing surfaces of blue, gray and green, or red. (Metalmarks get their name from their shiny metallic spots or checks, although some species lack these markings.)

Some species of metalmarks display unusual butterfly behavior. The Mormon Metalmark (*Apodemia mormo*), for example, with a distinctive pattern of white squares on its dark wings, perches upside down in direct sun.

The forelegs of the male metalmarks are shortened, but are of normal length in the female. The club of the antenna is often pointed. Metalmark eggs are somewhat flat and may have fine lines etched on the surface. The green or whitish caterpillars are also flattened but plump, and frequently very hairy. Some tropical species have brilliantly colored knobs. The caterpillars feed on an extremely wide variety of plants, but little is known about the specific food plants of this distinctive family. The downy chrysalises also vary widely; some hang freely by the tails from host plants, while others are attached with silk to the surfaces of leaves.

In North America, a number of swamp and dune species are endangered by development. Lange's Metalmark (*Apodemia mormo langei*), one of several subspecies of the Mormon, has been designated as Endangered and survives only in an isolated coastal dune habitat east of Antioch, California.

The Swamp Metalmark (*Calephelis muticum*), like all metalmarks, gets its name from shiny metallic spots on the upper wing surfaces. (Ray Coleman)

LIBYTHEIDAE
THE SNOUT BUTTERFLIES

The Snout Butterfly
(*Libytheana bachmanii*).
(Jeff Lepore)

Butterflies belonging to the Libytheidae, although the smallest of all butterfly families, are found on every continent. The family is composed of only a dozen species around the world, only two of which are found in North America.

With their long, beaklike palpi and squared-off forewings, snouts are easily recognized. The extremely elongated labial palps serve no obvious specialized function, but give these butterflies an aerodynamic look. This is a very old butterfly family; imprints of snouts, along with leaves of their host plant, the hackberry, have been found in shales some 30 million years old.

They are fairly uniform in size, with a wingspan of about 1 5/8 to 1 7/8 inches. The squared tips of the

forewings extend well beyond the hind wings. The forelegs are shortened in the male, but in the female they are well developed.

The North American species are mottled autumnal colors, unlike their tropical Asian relatives which are brighter, some showing beautiful suffusions of colors.

The eggs are oval, with delicate, paired ribs. The caterpillars are green, covered with short hairs and swollen in the first segments.

The angular, green chrysalis overwinters, suspended by its tail from the leaves of the caterpillar's host plant.

Only two species are found in North America. Although its residence is in the South, the Snout

53

Butterfly (*Libytheana bachmanii*) is found from the states of the Great Lakes, east to New England, south through the Rockies, all the way down into Arizona, southern California, and Mexico. The Southern or Mexican Snout (*Libytheana carinenta*) is found from Texas and Arizona to Paraguay.

Both species favor nectar from peach, dogwood, and rabbit brush. Both also are known for their long migratory flights in which millions of butterflies fly far north of their normal southerly range. The Southern Snout has, surprisingly, been found as far north as Kansas.

The Southern Snout Butterfly (*Libytheana carimenta*) has a distinctive beaklike palpi. (Joe DiStefano)

NYMPHALIDAE
BRUSH-FOOTED BUTTERFLIES

The Meadow Fritillary
(*Clossiana bellona*).
(Guy Gillette)

One of the largest and most diverse families—approximately three thousand species worldwide—brush-footed butterflies can be found all over the world. About one hundred and sixty species can be found at various times in North America, either as permanent residents or visiting strays.

Some of the most brilliantly colored butterflies belong to this family, and the range of pattern and wing shape is extensive. Several of the larger groups are known around the world by their popular names —Admirals (Limenitini), Vanessas or Painted Ladies (Vanessidi), and Fritillaries (Argynnini).

Two important subfamilies—the longwings (Heliconiinae) and the hackberries (Apaturinae)—are also included here. This diverse family also includes the checkerspots, crescentspots, anglewings, leafwings, and tortoiseshells.

Many Nymphalidae found in North America are some shade of orange. They are often medium-sized, with wing spans of 1½ to 3 inches, although there are both smaller and larger brush-foots in a wide spectrum of colors and a variety of shapes. (The longwings tend to be larger, and the checkerspots and crescentspots smaller.)

Both male and female Nymphalidae have reduced forelegs which are useless for walking. These forelegs give the family its common name of brush-foot. Brush-footed butterflies also have large knobs on their antennae and furry palpi. They often perch with their wings half open.

55

Brush-foot eggs vary greatly, although the surface is frequently ribbed, and these ribs are sometimes extended into points.

Caterpillars of most groups within the family are usually spiny, although some are smooth-skinned, with points only at the head and/or tail.

The chrysalises are usually spiked and angled, hanging upside down from silken pads. Most species overwinter as caterpillars or chrysalises, although tortoiseshells and anglewings overwinter as adults.

The host plants for the caterpillars range from trees, shrubs, and vines to wild and cultivated herbaceous plants.

Most Nymphalidae are powerful fliers and have strong territorial instincts. Several species of painted ladies are notable travelers, invading the North in impressive numbers each year.

Other species have extremely wide ranges, and some are found throughout the Americas. The most exotic species of Nymphalidae are found in South and Central America and Mexico. A few of these stray into Texas every year.

Within the family, certain groups have famous characteristics. The anglewings—which include the commas, question marks, and tortoiseshells—fold their bright wings to show murky undersides that completely blend with their surroundings, making them superior camouflagers.

The caterpillars of the longwings feed on poisonous passionflower vines, rendering themselves a nasty mouthful for predators. Other species merely mimic the appearance of the poisonous types, thereby gaining protection by association.

Here are some of the rarest—and also some of the most abundant—species of the family Nymphalidae.

ADMIRALS (Limenitini)

Most admirals and sisters can be recognized by the large white V design. The name "Admiral" does not refer to the crisp, military look of their banded wings, but rather it is a corruption of "Admirable," an older name for these butterflies that Vladimir Nabokov often used.

Admiral caterpillars often develop in two stages. When cold weather comes on, they roll up leaves, tuck themselves inside, and tie the bases with silk. Here they hibernate for the winter. In spring, hungry caterpillars emerge and continue their development.

The admirals and their numerous allies are represented in all regions and include many confusingly similar species. Each of the several American species occupies only one section of the continent. Only the Viceroy (*Basilarchia archippus*) occupies all of North America.

Throughout the Rocky Mountains Weidemeyer's Admiral (*Basilarchia weidemeyerii*), with its coal-black wings crossed by broad, white bands, is the only banded admiral.

The White Admiral or "Banded Purple" (*Basilarchia arthemis*) dwells primarily in the Northeast. The Red-spotted Purple (*Basilarchia astyanax*) is found in the Southeast and Lorquin's Admiral (*Basilarchia lorquini*) flies on the West Coast.

Along the northern edge of its range, the Red-spotted Purple, which is solid black with a shimmering blue-green iridescence over its hind wings, may hybridize with the White Admiral, which has a milk-white band across the middle of its wings. The result of this interbreeding is a partially banded offspring.

The Red-spotted Purple gains protection from predators by copying the appearance of the toxic blue Pipevine Swallowtail, although it lacks the tails that distinguish the Pipevine.

The upper surface of the spectacular California Sister (*Adelpha bredowii*) is dark brown, narrowly banded with white. Underneath, its wings are complexly marked with auburn, pale blue, orange, and white bands and spots. The California Sister flies in the oak groves of mountains and along the coast and offshore islands of Washington and California, east through Nevada and Arizona, and into Colorado and New Mexico. Its relative, the Mexican Sister,

The innocent Viceroy *(Basilarchia archippus)*, above, mimics the poisonous Monarch butterfly. (Ray Gilbert)

The Weidemeyers Admiral *(Basilarchia weidemeyerii)*, below, shows a large white V design typical of many admirals. (R.J. Erwin)

The Red-spotted Purple (*Basilarchia astyanax*) looks like the toxic Pipevine Swallowtail. (L. West)

may be found in the Rio Grande Valley, along the Texas-Mexico border.

PAINTED LADIES (Vanessidi)

Vanessas, or painted ladies, are widely distributed and include that most cosmopolitan of butterflies, the Painted Lady (*Vanessa cardui*), perhaps the most widespread butterfly in the world. Painted ladies are found throughout Africa, Europe, and Asia, as well as in North America. Painted ladies fly year-round in the Sonoran deserts and possibly some other warm regions. In most parts of the country, however, they disappear with the first hard frost. In February and March, painted ladies begin immigrating from the Southwest, infiltrating the Northeast, and by late spring they have repopulated the continent. This

trip is one-way only, and the number of immigrants fluctuates from year to year.

There are three species of painted lady in North America. They are the Painted Lady (*Vanessa cardui*), the American Painted Lady (*Vanessa virginiensis*), and the West Coast Lady (*Vanessa annabella*). *Vanessa cardui* flies throughout North America, from the sub-Arctic south to Panama. Its upper wing surfaces are salmon-orange with black blotches, the black forewing tips spattered with clear white spots. Underneath, the forewing is predominately rosy pink, with an olive, black, and white pattern.

The Red Admiral (*Vanessa atalanta*), although a relative, is not a painted lady in the strictest sense of the term. This *Vanessa* has black wings barred with

The American Painted Lady (*Vanessa virginiensis*), right, is one of three painted ladies found in North America. (Ray Coleman)

58

bright red, with a sprinkling of white dots on the tips. This is an unmistakable butterfly seen in gardens and fields all over North America.

This theatrical butterfly is easy to approach, and seems quite sociable with humans. It is not unusual to find Red Admirals flying with painted ladies in midsummer.

The Red Admiral is usually a summer resident in the North, either dying out or returning South in the fall.

FRITILLARIES (Argynnini)

The big, beautiful fritillaries, known for their tawny-orange wings that bear many black zigzags, dots, crescents, and bars, are among the most abundant butterflies in the United States. There are at least thirty different species of fritillary flying in nearly every possible kind of habitat.

The Diana (*Speyeria diana*), its dark wings swathed in brilliant orange, spans nearly 4 inches across, making it the largest and certainly one of the most beautiful fritillaries. The female has completely different coloring. The female Diana is blue and mimics the poisonous Pipevine Swallowtail. The Diana has a considerable range, from Maryland and western Pennsylvania, west to Oklahoma, and south to Louisiana.

The smaller, low-flying Meadow Fritillary (*Clossiana bellona*) is one of the most abundant bog fritillaries, particularly in the East. It flaps its richly patterned gold and black wings rapidly and flies with a zigzag motion.

The Red Admiral *(Vanessa atalanta)* has unmistakable red bars across its wings. (Michael Lustbader)

The male Diana *(Speyeria diana).*
(Kjell B. Sandved)

CHECKERSPOTS AND CRESCENTSPOTS

There may be as many as two dozen different species of checkerspots in North America, some very similar in appearance. Their wings are usually black above, with various combinations of cream-colored and red or orange dots. Below, the wings are usually a paler orange with cream-colored spots and black veins. Like other externally similar butterflies, checkerspots are believed to give off scents, called pheromones, which may help members of each species recognize each other. Checkerspots are usually small and are seldom adventuresome flyers. Yet they are found in every corner of North America and in virtually every habitat.

ANGLEWINGS AND TORTOISESHELLS

These butterflies have irregular, somewhat ragged wing borders. When the wings are folded at rest, the drab undersides resemble leaves or pieces of bark, making them difficult to see. The uppersides tend to be somewhat brighter shades of orange and rust-brown. This group includes anglewings, tortoiseshells, commas, question marks, leafwings, and daggerwings.

The small, bright Milbert's Tortoiseshell *(Aglais milberti)* flies in many altitudes and climates throughout the United States. This butterfly is so versatile that it can thrive in every kind of habitat, from desert to rain forest to alpine summit. Milbert's Tor-

61

Harris' Checkerspot *(Charidryas harrisii)*, above, and the Colon or "Snowberry" Checkerspot *(Euphydryas colon)*, left, display contrasting wing surfaces typical of these butterflies: black above with orange checks and dots; pale below with black veins and creamy spots. (Above, L. West. Left, Tom and Pat Leeson)

The bright wings of Milbert's Tortoiseshell *(Aglais milberti)* have a dark brown border with blue bars. (Alvin E. Staffan)

toiseshell may sometimes be seen even in midwinter in many temperate areas.

HACKBERRIES (Apaturinae)

Apaturinae is a subfamily of Nymphalidae. The wings of these lovely butterflies are complexly marked above and richly patterned below.

The Hackberry butterflies have recently been divided into three main groups: those related to the Hackberry Emperor *(Asterocampa celtis)*, to the Empress Leilia *(Asterocampa leilia)*, and to the Tawny Emperor *(Asterocampa clyton)*.

The males of the Hackberry Emperor exhibit the beautiful structural coloration that all the emperors are known for, best seen when the insects are viewed at an angle. This butterfly flies from Canada to the Dakotas, east to Massachusetts, south to Florida and

Texas. The Florida population of the Hackberry Emperor is sometimes mistakenly called the Empress Alicia, but Alicia is larger.

LONGWINGS (Heliconiinae)

Heliconiinae is a subfamily of Nymphalidae. Among the most beautifully colored butterflies, seventy species occur in Central and South America, with a scant three or four found in the southern United States. Some of these are common and plentiful in South America; others are extremely rare and even today are known from only a few specimens.

The longwings are characterized by their narrow wings, long antennae, and thin, elongated abdomen. In size they are remarkably uniform, ranging from about 3 to 35/8 inches. The longwings are thought to be unpalatable to predators because their caterpillars

The magnificent Julia (*Dryas julia*) may have a wingspan of
3¹/₂ inches or more. Underneath, the wings are much lighter
in color with a silver streak on the hindwing.
(Kjell B. Sandved)

feed on poisonous passionflower vines. They advertise their distastefulness with brilliant colors, com-
bining black with red, orange, yellow, and blue in
distinctive patterns.

Enormous variation within individual species
makes this one of the most confusing groups to identify. Several other species and genera mimic the patterns of the longwings to fool their predators and
gain similar protection.

Many longwings, such as the Zebra Longwing
(*Heliconius charitonius*), reproduce continuously, feeding on rich concentrations of pollen, which provides
protein for long-term egg production. Most long-

wing species are long-lived and tend to exist in large
populations. Longwings fly slowly, almost lazily.
They congregate together during the day and sleep
together at night in large clusters hanging from
shrubs.

These butterflies have very large heads and eyes
and are thought to have an extremely wide field of
vision. The eggs are of a peculiar bottle shape and
are laid singly. The caterpillars are often dark-
colored, hump-backed, armed with long spurs and
spines, or vividly colored, imitating other caterpillars. The chrysalis is suspended, head down, from
the stem of the host plant.

JULIA (*Dryas iulia*)

The long, narrow wings of the male Julia are a clear bright orange, the female a duller orange-brown. Black bars and margins may be pronounced or missing. Underneath, both sexes are tan with a silver streak on the upper edge of the hind wing. The Julia is a more vigorous flyer than some other longwings, but stops frequently at flowers and is easily observed. The Julia is often abundant in the Florida Keys and is also found in other parts of southern Florida and southern Texas.

ZEBRA LONGWING
(*Heliconius charitonius*)

Both sides of the Zebra Longwing's wings are jet black, banded with lemon-yellow. Near the base of the underwing is a cluster of small, crimson spots.

The Zebra Longwings are not strong flyers. They tend to flap their long, narrow wings slowly and awkwardly. At sundown they gather together and rest in large groups. In warmer months, these dramatic butterflies are found in many parts of the South and Southwest, wandering from Florida and Texas to

The Zebra Longwing (*Heliconius charitonius*) advertises itself with dramatic stripes. Like all longwing species, this butterfly is distasteful to predators because its caterpillars feed on poisonous passionflower vines. (Kjell B. Sandved)

South Carolina, southern California, Colorado, and the Great Plains. They can be seen year-round in Florida's Everglades National Park.

CRIMSON-PATCHED LONGWING
(Heliconius erato)

The long, narrow wings of the Crimson-patched Longwing are rounded at the tips. Both sides of the wings are black, crossed by a broad, crimson patch on the forewing and a narrow, yellow line on the hind wing line. The coloring below is slightly less vivid.

Like other species of longwings, the Crimson-patched Longwing is a relatively poor flyer, but what it lacks in speed and agility, it more than makes up for in sheer beauty and theatrical coloring. Unfortunately for North American butterfly lovers, the Crimson-patched Longwing is seen only in very warm climates from southern Texas through Mexico to South America.

Despite its enormous wingspan, the Crimson-patched Longwing (Heliconius erato) is a relatively slow, lazy flier. (W.K. Fletcher)

SATYRIDAE
SATYRS OR BROWNS

The Appalachin Brown
(Satyrodes appalachia).
(L. West)

Only about fifty of the three thousand known species of Satyridae are found in North America. Most seem to be simple shades of brown and gray, yet when closely observed their muted colors are quite complex. Although most are similar in appearances, their size varies considerably, their wings spanning anywhere from 1 to 27/8 inches. One characteristic feature shared by all species is their large eyespots, which serve as diversionary targets to keep predators from attacking their bodies.

The eggs of the Satyridae are generally dome-shaped and delicately ribbed. The green-striped caterpillars are usually smooth, with a more or less developed forked tail. Most feed on grasses or canes and overwinter; the Arctic species sometimes take two summers to reach maturity.

The brown or green chrysalises are round and smooth; they hang by their tails from grass stems or tuck into the base of grass, among leaf litter, or under stones.

Like the brush-foots, satyrs have reduced forelegs. The satyrs, however, have swollen veins at the base of the forewings.

Some species of satyrs can be found in virtually every habitat and every altitude, wherever there is grass: woods and meadows, mountains and open tundra. One of the most common mountain species, the California Arctic, can be seen within the city limits of San Francisco. They also enjoy every kind of weather. Some species like sun, others prefer shade. Some even fly after sundown, when they are often mistaken for moths.

The Little Wood Satyr (Megisto cymela), which is actually larger than most small satyrs, is a prolific and hardy species that can readily adapt to changes in its environment, making it one of the most abundant satyrs.

Most adult satyrs, however, usually stay close to home, dancing between grass blades and tree trunks. The Appalachin Brown (Satyrodes appalachia) dwells in damp, brushy marshes from Maine south through the Appalachians to Mississippi and central Florida. It is fairly fragile and unable to adapt to changes in its wetland habitat.

The Large Wood Nymph (Cercyonic pegala), with a wingspan of between 2 and 2⅞ inches, is the largest species of wood nymph. It can be found everywhere in North America, but the protective coloration of its wings blends imperceptibly with bark, making it hard to see. Its color varies from light brown to deep chocolate-brown above, much lighter below with large, black eyespots often rimmed with yellow.

The Large Wood Nymph (Cercyonis pegala) shows the dark, muted coloring and pattern typical of the family Satyridae. (Kjell B. Sandved)

DANAIDAE
MILKWEED BUTTERFLIES

The Monarch
(*Danaus plexippus*).
(Robert Bright)

Although this family contains the familiar Monarch, most of its three hundred species are found in tropical Asia. Only four of them are found in North America.

The large North American species have wingspans between 3 and 4 inches. Many tropical milkweed butterflies are even larger. Their wings are burnt-orange, with dark veins and white spots. The milkweed butterflies include one of the most famous butterfly migrants—the Monarch (*Danaus plexippus*).

Because the caterpillars feed on toxic milkweeds, the adult butterflies contain noxious body fluids which make them distasteful to birds. Consequently, the Viceroy and many other nonpoisonous butterfly groups mimic their coloring.

The eggs are domed, with prominent ribbing. The caterpillars are smooth-skinned with bright body striping. Pairs of long filaments dangle from head and tail, giving them an aggressive appearance. The waxy chrysalises are rounded, decorated with gold or silver spots. Each hangs suspended head down from a thin, silk pad.

All milkweed butterflies are strong, vigorous flyers, but none is more exuberant than the Monarch.

MONARCH (*Danaus plexippus*)

The remarkable Monarch is native to North and South America, but has colonized Australia and the Hawaiian Islands. It also occurs as a stray in Europe.

The Monarch is very large, with a wingspan up to 4 inches. The wings are bright burnt-orange above with black veins and black margins spattered with white. The tip of the forewing is black, with large white and orange spots. The underwing is a paler orange. The female Monarch is darker and the black veins on her wings are less clearly defined.

For sustained flight over long periods this famous migrant has no rival among butterflies. (A marked Monarch was recovered 77 miles away from the site of its original capture on the same day.) The Monarch is the only butterfly that migrates both north and south on a regular basis each year.

In North America the Monarch is present only during the summer. Toward summer's end, the butterflies begin to move south, initially in small groups, and then in masses of tens of thousands. The western populations fly southwest, hibernating in small areas along the Pacific coast of California. The eastern populations fly south or south-southwest, disappearing at the border of Mexico. Their mysterious winter quarters were recently discovered in a small valley high in the Sierra Madre of middle Mexico. In an area less than 4 acres, an estimated 14 million Monarchs were found packed together on tree trunks and branches.

In the spring, Monarchs fly north again to reoccupy the vast area that they abandoned the previous autumn. On the return flight, they halt to deposit eggs on any milkweeds that they come across. The returning butterflies are usually members of several generations, although occasionally a single individual makes the entire round-trip journey.

QUEEN (*Danaus gilippus*)

Smaller than the Monarch, but still a big butterfly with a wingspan up to 3⅜ inches, the Queen is deep reddish brown with black margins and black veins. Fine white dots are sprinkled along the margins on both sides of the wings, with larger dots on the tips of the forewings. Males have sex pouches on the hind wings and brushlike hair pencils within the abdomen. In courtship, the male Queen extends these brushes to release scents that attract the female.

The Queen cannot tolerate cold. Temporary migrations may account for the presence of this butterfly in the northwestern United States, but its usual range is distinctly southerly, from Nevada and southern California east to Texas, around the Gulf of Mexico to Florida and southern Georgia.

The Queen *(Danaus gilippus)*, right, is one of only four species of milkweed butterflies found in North America. (Stephen Dalton)

HESPERIIDAE
SKIPPERS

The Delaware Skipper
(*Atrytone delaware*).
(Pat Lynch)

There are approximately three thousand species of Hesperiidae worldwide and about two hundred and fifty are known in North America. These butterflies derive their popular name from their darting, skipping flight, which is unlike any other butterfly's. They are seldom found at higher altitudes. Skippers resemble moths, with their thick, hairy bodies and triangular wings. Some skippers rest with their wings folded flat over the body, but others hold their wings straight out to the sides and their front wings upward at an angle. The coloring of most species is subdued, running chiefly to various shades of brown and gold, with lighter markings.

The Juba Skipper (*Hesperia juba*), left, has the stout, hairy body and triangular wings typical of all skippers. (W.K. Fletcher)

Skippers are small to medium-sized, with wingspans measuring between 1/2 inch and 2 1/2 inches. They have proportionately larger bodies and smaller wings than other butterflies.

The eggs are oval, very small (less than 1/256 of an inch wide), with flattened bases that may be smooth or ribbed. Most skipper caterpillars are stout, green, and tapered, with large heads. Many feed on grasses. They live protected by leaves, which they weave together with silken threads to create shelters for themselves. When they are ready to pupate, the caterpillars often weave loose cocoons. The smooth chrysalises are often covered with a waxy powder, and the head ends may be pointed. Both caterpillar and chrysalis may overwinter.

Skippers fall into three subfamilies: Hisperiinae, Pyrginae, and Pyrrhopyginae.

73

Like other folded-wing skippers, the Saltmarsh *(Panoquina panoquin)* rests its forewings and hind wings at different angles. (Ken Brate)

FOLDED WING (Hisperiinae)

Tawny orange or brown skippers belong to the Hisperiinae. When at rest, these skippers fold their forewings and hind wings at different angles.

Like many species of butterfly, the Salt Marsh *(Panoquina panoquin)* is found only in one particular habitat—salt marshes or tidal marshes and meadows along the east coast, from Connecticut to southern Florida, then west along the Gulf coast to Mississippi.

The Juba Skipper *(Hesperia juba)* and the Delaware Skipper *(Atrytone delaware)* are more versatile and widespread. The Juba Skipper seeks concentrated sources of moisture and nectar in the gullies and canyons of the drier mountains from British Columbia south along the coast to the Great Basin and the Rockies. The Delaware Skipper inhabits the open woods and grassy lowlands, from Massachusetts south to Florida and Texas, west to Minnesota and the eastern foothills of the Rockies.

The large Golden Skipper *(Poanes taxiles)* is a brighter, brassier color than most skippers. It is the only skipper that lives in the west, found in dark gullies and valleys from Nebraska south and west to Arizona. Unlike most butterflies, the Golden Skipper prefers shade to sun, and flies joyfully on overcast days.

The Hobomok *(Poanes hobomok)* is widespread in eastern North America, and is even found within the city limits of New York. But this is one common skipper that is also comfortable at higher altitudes. A few Hobomok colonies occur in the Sangre de Cristo mountains of Colorado at higher elevations than is normal for the species.

SPREAD WINGED (Pyrginae)

These skippers, which may be dark, checkered, and long-tailed, comprise the subfamily Pyrginae. They tend to bask with wings spread open or partly open. The United States is home to many long-tailed skippers, including the widespread *Urbanus proteus.* This lovely butterfly, with its velvety brown wings and iridescent blue body, is a resident of southern Cali-

The Golden Skipper *(Poanes taxile)* flies in the western United States. (R.J. Erwin)

fornia, Arizona, Texas, and Florida, where it is considered a pest by farmers, who call it the "Bean-leaf Roller" because of its appetite for legumes and crucifers. The species is often abundant, and population pressures lead to sometimes huge migrations into northern states during late summer.

The Common Checkered Skipper (Pyrgus communis), with its pattern of small white checkering over black wings, may be the most common skipper in North America. Because this species thrives on hollyhock, hibiscus, or cheeseweed, it is found throughout North America, although it is seldom seen in the northern states.

Horace's Duskywing (Erynnis horatius) enjoys the warm, sunny spots in clearings or along the edges of woodlands. This butterfly has managed to adapt itself to the destruction of its primary habitat and can thrive in road cuts and powerline rights-of-way, as long as herbicides were not used to destroy plant growth.

The Silver-spotted Skipper (Epargyreus clarus) is named for the large, glassy patch of silver on its hind wing. This skipper has one of the most extensive ranges of any North American butterfly, adapting itself readily to suburbs and city parks from the Pacific to Atlantic coasts.

The Long-tailed Skipper
(*Urbanus proteus*), left, and the
Common Checkered Skipper
(*Pyrgus communis*), right, bask
with their wings partly open.
(Left: J.H. Robinson.
Right: Gerald Ray Konslek)

Horace's Duskywing (*Erynnis
horatius*), below, is highly
adaptable.
(Ken Brate)

PYRRHOPYGINAE

The third subfamily of skippers is a colorful subtropical group known for their scarlet-spotted bodies and glistening blue wings. In North America, however, only a single species of Pyrrhopyginae, a much less vibrant representative than its tropical relatives, is found. The Araxes Skipper (*Pyrrhopyge araxes*) is quite large (up to 2½ inches in wing span), with glassy white spots on its brown upper wing surfaces. To add some dash to its otherwise muted coloring, its wings have a brown and white checked fringe.

GIANT SKIPPER (Megathyminae)

Among the most unusual skippers are the large American Megathyminae—giant skippers—which are sometimes classified as a separate family. In their black and gold coloring, the giants are similar to other skippers. But in size and shape they are quite different. (Their heads are narrower than the thorax, and their antennae have rounded tips.) Giant skippers have large, powerful wings—the wingspan of the largest exceeds 3 inches—which makes them fast, strong fliers. Their speed makes them difficult to observe. There are thought to be twenty to fifty species, most of them in the American Southwest and Mexico.

The egg is flattish with indented edges and is laid on the agave or yucca. The whitish caterpillars feed on the leaves and roots of the yucca, agave, and manfreda. (These are the cactus from which tequilla and mescal are made. Mescal is not considered authentic unless this caterpillar is in the bottle.)

Caterpillars bore into the fleshy leaves, stems, or roots of the host plant, hollowing out chambers which they later line with silk and close with "trap" doors. Enclosing themselves inside the chambers, the caterpillars pupate. When metamorphosis is complete, the adult butterfly re-emerges through the trap door.

The Silver-spotted Skipper (*Epargyreus clarus*) is identified by a glassy patch on its hind wing. (R.J. Erwin)

INDEX OF BUTTERFLIES

Page numbers in **boldface** refer to illustrations.

Acadian Hairstreak (*Satyrium acadica*), 19
Acmon Blue (*Icaricia acmon*), 46, **47**
Admirals (*Limenitini*), 56–58, **57**
Alaskan Swallowtail (*Papilio machaon*), 28, **29**
Alfalfa (*Colias eurytheme*), 38, **38**
American Megathyminae, 78
American Painted Lady (*Vanessa virginiensis*), 58, **59**
Anglewings, 61, 63
Anise Swallowtail (*Papilio zelicaon*), 28; caterpillar, **10**
Apollos (*Parnassius*), 31–33
Appalachin Brown (*Satyrodes appalachia*), **67**, 68
Araxes Skipper (*Pyrrhopyge araxes*), 78
Australasian Birdwing (*Ornithoptera*), 27

Banded Purple (*Basilarchia arthemis*), 56
Bean-leaf Roller (*Urbanus proteus*), 75–76, **76**
Black Swallowtail (*Papilio*), 28
Blue Wing (*Myscelia ethusa*), 20
Blues (*Polyommatinae*), 46–49
Bluish Green Hairstreak (*Callophrys viridis*), 25
Brimstones (*Coliadinae*), 37–40
Brown Elfin (*Incisalia augustinus*), 43–44, **45**
Browns (*Satyridae*), 67–68
Brush-footed (*Nymphalidae*), 55–66
Buckeye (*Junonia coenia*), 20, 25, **26**

Cabbage White (*Artogeia rapae*), **34**, 36–37
Calephelis, 51
California Arctic, 67
California Dogface (*Zerene eurydice*), 18–19, 40, **40**
California Patch (*Chlosyne californica*), 19

California Sister (*Adelpha bredowii*), 56
California Xerces Blue, 25
Checkerspots, 61, **62**
Clodius Parnassian (*Parnassius clodius*), **6**, 31–32, **33**
Clouded Sulphur (*Colias philodice*), **37**, 38
Cloudless Giant Sulphur (*Phoebis sennae*), 24
Colon Checkerspot (*Euphydryas colon*), **62**
Colorado Hairstreak (*Hypaurotis crysalus*), **41**, 43
Comma (*Polygonia comma*), 21, **23**
Common Checkered Skipper (*Pyrgus communis*), 76, **77**
Common Sulphur (*Colias philodice*), **37**, 38
Compton Tortoiseshell (*Nymphalis vau-album*), 20
Coppers (*Lycaeninae*), 49–50
Coral Hairstreak (*Harkenclenus titus*), 45, **46**
Crescentspots, 61
Crimson-patched Longwing (*Heliconius erato*), 66, **66**

Danaidae, 69–71
Delaware Skipper (*Atrytone delaware*), **73**, 74
Desert Green Hairstreak (*Callophrys comstocki*), 19
Diana (*Speyeria diana*), 60, **61**
Dogface (*Zerene cesonia*), 40
Dorcas Copper (*Epidemia dorcas*), 20
Dragontail (*Lamproptera*), 27

Eastern Black Swallowtail (*Papilio polyxenes*), **27**, 28
Eastern Tailed Blue (*Everes comyntas*), 46–47, **48**
Edwards' Hairstreak (*Satyrium edwardsii*), 19
Emerald-studded Blue (*Icaricia acmon*), 46, **47**
Empress Alicia, 63
Empress Leilia (*Asterocampa leilia*), 63

Fatal Metalmark (*Calephelis nemesis*), **51**
Flying Pansy (*Colias eurydice*), 40, **40**
Folded Wing Skippers (*Hisperiinae*), 74–75
Fritillaries (*Argynnini*), **17**, 18, 25, **55**, 60

Giant Skipper (*Megathyminae*), 78
Giant Swallowtail (*Heraclides*), 28–30, **29**
Golden Skipper (*Poanes taxiles*), 74–75, **75**
Gorgon Copper (*Gaeides gorgon*), 16–17
Gossamer wings (*Lycaenidae*), 41–50
Great Southern White (*Ascia monuste*), **35**, 37
Great Spangled Fritillary (*Speyeria cybele*), 18, **19**
Gulf Fritillary (*Agraulis vanillae*), **17**

Hackberries (*Apaturinae*), 63
Hairstreaks (*Theclinae*), 19, 25, **41**, 43–45, **46**
Harris' Checkerspot (*Charidryas harrisii*), **62**
Harvester (*Feniseca tarquinius*), 10, 42–43, **42**
Hesperiidae, 73–78
Horace's Duskywing (*Erynnis horatius*), 76, **77**

Juba Skipper (*Hesperia juba*), **72**, 74
Julia (*Dryas julia*), **64**, 65

Lange's Metalmark (*Apodemia mormo langei*), 52
Large Wood Nymph (*Cercyonic pegala*), 68, **68**
Libytheidae, 53–54
Little Wood Satyr (*Megisto cymela*), 68
Long-tailed Skipper (*Urbanus proteus*), 75–76, **76**
Longwings (*Heliconiinae*), 63–64, 65–66, **65**, **66**

Lorquin's Admiral (*Basilarchia lorquini*), 56
Lycaenidae, 41–50

Malachite (*Siproeta stelenes*), 12, 20
Marblewings, 36
Meadow Fritillary (*Clossiana bellona*), **55**, 60
Metalmarks, 51–52
Mexican Sister, 56, 58
Mexican Snout (*Libytheana carinenta*), 54, **54**
Milbert's Tortoiseshell (*Aglais milberti*), 20, 61, 63, **63**
Milkweeds (*Danaidae*), 69–71
Mimic (*Hypolimnas misippus*), 17, **18**
Monarch (*Danaus plexippus*), 69–70, **69**
   caterpillars of, 10
   life cycle of, **12–13**
   migration of, 24–25, **24**
   Viceroy and, 22, **57**
Mormon Metalmark (*Apodemia mormo*), 51, 52
Mourning Cloak (*Nymphalis antiopa*), 21, **22**

Nivalis Copper (*Epidemia nivalis*), 12, **14**, 17
Nymphalidae, 15, 55–66

Oarisma edwardsii, 25
Old World Swallowtail (*Papilio machaon*), 28, **29**
Orange Dog (*Heraclides cresphontes*), 28–30, **29**
Orange Sulphur (*Colias eurytheme*), 38, **38**
Orange-barred Giant Sulphur (*Phoebis philea*), 39, 40
Orangetips (*Pieriniae*), 37

Painted Ladies (*Vanessidi*), 58–60
Painted Lady (*Vanessa cardui*), 22, 24, 58
Palaeno Sulphur (*Colias palaeno*), 20

Papilionidae, 27–33
Parnassians, **7**, 31–33
Pavon (*Doxocopa pavon*), 20
Pearly Crescentspot (*Phyciodes tharos*), 18
Phoebises, **16**
Phoebus Parnassian (*Parnassius phoebus*), 32, **32**
Pieridae, 35–40
Pipevine Swallowtail (*Battus*), 30–31, 56, 58, 60
Purplish Copper (*Epidemia helloides*), 50, **50**
Pyrrhopyginae, 78

Queen (*Danaus gilippus*), 22, 70–71, **71**
Question Mark (*Polygonia interrogationis*), 21–22

Red Admiral (*Vanessa atalanta*), 58, 60, **60**
Red-banded Hairstreak (*Calycopis cecrops*), 43, **44**
Red-spotted Purple (*Basilarchia astyanax*), 56, **58**
Regal Fritillary (*Speyeria idalia*), 25
Riodinida, 51–52
Ruddy Daggerwing (*Marpesia petreus*), **7**, 2¹

Saltmarsh (*Panoquina panoquin*), 74, **74**
Sara Orangetip (*Anthocharis sara*), 35, **36**, 37
Satyridae, 67–68
Silver-spotted Skipper (*Epargyreus clarus*), 76, **78**
Silvery Blue (*Glaucopsyche lygdamus*), 47, 49, **49**
Skippers (*Hesperiidae*), **72**, 73–78
Small White (*Artogeia rapae*), 36–37
Snouts (*libytheana bachmanii*), 53–54, **53**
Snowberry Checkerspot (*Euphydryas colon*), **62**

Southern Snout (*Libytheana carinenta*), 54, **54**
Spicebush Tiger Swallowtail (*Pterourus troilus*), 30, **31**
Spread-Winged Skippers (*Pyrginae*), 75–77
Sulphurs (*Coliadinae*), 20, **21**, 24, 3⁷–40
Swallowtails, 15, 27–31, 56, 58, 60
Swamp Metalmark (*Calephelis muticum*), 51, **52**

Tawny Emperor (*Asterocampa clyton*), 63
Thoas Swallowtail (*Heraclides thoas*), 28
Tiger Swallowtail (*Papilio glaucus*), caterpillar, **10**
Tiger Swallowtail (*Pterourus glaucus*), 28, 30, **30**
Tortoiseshells, 61, 63

Viceroy (*Basilarchia archippus*), 22, 56, **57**, 69

Weidemeyer's Admiral (*Basilarchia weidemeyerii*), 56, **57**
West Coast Lady (*Vanessa annabella*), 58
West Indian Buckeye (*Junonia evarete*), 20
Western Black Swallowtail, 28
White Admiral (*Basilarchia arthemis*), 56
White Peacock (*Anartia jatrophae*), 20
White-angled Sulphur (*Anteos clorinde*), 39, 40
Whites (*Pieriniae*), 36–37
Woodland Skipper (*Ochlodes sylvanoides*), **9**

Xerces Blue (*Blaucopsyche xerces*), 25

Zebra Longwing (*Heliconius charitonius*), 64, 65–66, **65**
Zebra Swallowtail (*Eurytides marcellus*), **15**, 31